Shape of Faith

OTHER BOOKS BY JOHN PHILLIPS

Language Is (Sardines Press, San Francisco, CA, 2005)
What Shape Sound (Skysill Press, Nottingham, 2011)
Heretic (Longhouse, Guilford, VT, 2016)

CHAPBOOKS

Instances (with Roger Snell) (Third Ear Books, 2000)
While (Longhouse, 2000)
Path (Longhouse, 2002)
A Small Window (Longhouse, 2005)
Soundless (Punch Press, 2007)
Pages (Country Valley Press, 2008)
Spell (Kater Murr's Press, 2009)
Fault (Kater Murr's Press, 2013)
This (Smallminded Books, 2016)

John Phillips

Shape of Faith

Shearsman Books

First published in the United Kingdom in 2017 by
Shearsman Books
50 Westons Hill Drive
Emersons Green
BRISTOL
BS16 7DF

Shearsman Books Ltd Registered Office
30–31 St. James Place, Mangotsfield, Bristol BS16 9JB
(this address not for correspondence)

www.shearsman.com

ISBN 978-1-84861-532-8

ACKNOWLEDGEMENTS

Many thanks to the editors of the following magazines and presses
where the majority of these poems first appeared: Analogue
Flashback Books, *The Cultural Society, Damn the Caesars, Dispatches
from the Poetry Wars, Dozen, First Intensity, Granite, Hassle,
Hummingbird, Kadar Koli, Litter Magazine,* Kater Murr's Press,
*Lallocropia, Longhouse, Murder of Krows, Noon, Otata, Persimmon,
Poetry Salzburg Review, Poetry Wales,* Punch Press, *Shearsman,*
Smallminded Books, *Stride, Strike* and *Tears in the Fence.*

Some were also in the following chapbooks and books: *This, Fault,
While, Plenty, Gone, Path, Language, The Healing Wound, Given,
Table Laid Bare, Instances* and *Heretic*; as well as the anthologies
Beyond Hepworth's Garden, Wave Hub and *Nerve Damage.*

Contents

for Jasna, Eva, Lana
& Roger Snell

LANGUAGE

Sometimes it
pretends to
deliver us
back beyond its
beginnings we
invent each time
it is used to

FAULT

That word you were going to say
the word you did say
wasn't quite the word you wanted to
something small
a fragment   fell from it
before you finished saying it
an invisible thing
that changed what you said,
that always changes it

RETURN

Each place is
another place

each time
you return.

To get where
you've been

never is
possible.

IF I REMEMBER

for Keith Waldrop

My daughter began to describe a room: books piled high in corners and a black iron bedstead. She even remembered the slightly acrid smell of stale pipe tobacco and how, on winter mornings, the heavy frost would make opening the one small window, high above the bed, difficult.

The room she described was the room in which my father had died; the house long since demolished.

Both events taking place several years before she was born.

RECOGNITION

Towards five
in the morning:
My hand creates
the words
I write,
the words I write
create me.

Day breaks in my body.

Each of us a sentence
in the process of being

said by someone who
doesn't know what

they are saying or why
they are saying it or

even whom it does or
does not concern

PARADISE

Because words reveal
the separation

of what is
from what is said to be:

in Paradise
language would be a sin.

LATEWORD

God not existing
proves what
to the contrary
worth doing
more than
steer clear of
History
yet to
unhappen

No matter
what it is
I'm doing

I've never yet
got over the
idea

I'm pretending
to do what
I am.

We look at what we think
is real knowing it is

only what we think it is
and any reality it might

have is a reality we have
made by thinking so. As if

we could do otherwise.

This coming
down to
being that
we are
here to
be incapable
fact of.

In a dark
in a darkened room there's a music

a music playing there
a woman slowly no
quickly passes she
into the room behind
dark in shadow the
dark

behind the music remains
doesn't quite remain it stays by going

she stays now gone still lingers his

lips to her music

the music is not dark it is
in a darkened room it makes not dark
gives a certain light to

light to the lips saying dark saying
light is a woman in the dark

music of a woman

a woman in a dark room of
light a woman

dark light

each in the other being one each other
one is more than oneself or is not

woman is a man loving the woman is a
man and woman loving a newborn daughter in the dark

light loving a child sung to

in a room darkened by dark
lips on lips   light
a certain music of

THIS

It is here you are
the very breath I

had to
pronounce it

WORDS

How suddenly
their being
there saying

whatever it is
they are saying
makes being here

listening have
the sense it
does without

which it would be
impossible
to face

everything no one
wants to
that we must

NINE MAIDENS

Circling
base of
stone standing
light
standing
rain
fallen
make light make stone
light
a stone light
it never is it
must be
cannot
fall and be
            let fall
stone
another
stone
standing
without
            passing
stone surrounds
                it
                is
not certain it is not
                    passing
                    stone
                    still
                    rain
                    light
                    standing

Of course
it won't be
the same
as silence

No one
would expect
it to
be or

even want
it so —
and yet
part of

me would
wish it
to mean
as much

What you are left with
when I have put down my pen
is different from what I
am left with.

HIS WORDS

for Gael Turnbull

Yesterday, reading your poems, I couldn't stop from shuffling
the words to one of them around:

ALWAYS

the lure of just
one poem more
as if the reshuffled
words might yet
reveal that whatever
it is we're
persisting for?

Became:

THAT

we're always
persisting for
the lure of
whatever the words
might reveal as if
yet one more
reshuffled poem
is just it.

Or, what might be worth saving:

HIS WORDS

Persisting for
the lure of
whatever words
might reveal.

LETTER

for Theodore Enslin

The daffodils are
just
    coming into
bloom
      Still
a number of
        croci
& a kind of blue
scilla
    I found
    years ago
in an
    abandoned garden
    a swallow just
      fluttered in

SACRIFICE

Thirty years ago, inside the cover of Dag Hammarskjöld's *Markings,* I wrote: *I know what to sacrifice.*

Now I wonder what it was — and if I did sacrifice it.

And whether I was right to.

AFTERWARDS

Every time I sit down
to write this

I expect someone else
to rise from my chair,

in a different world,
impossibly better.

AS

meaningless
the sun
means
us

MARGIN

I

Remembering
not re-
membered
ear hearing
not said
known stillness
unknown still
table bare
light shape of
window a table is
music not music
moment momentarily
bearing light
a chair alone
against table
light perceived
pattern passing
through light
door closed fast
against music
seeing sound
brightens edges
light
      remembered
fading
into

II

It will fall
fallen shadow
shadow fall
in the window
light does not
shadow table
fallen light
not sight
music
not memory
to remember
table bare
cluttered light
objects are
sound shifting
light around
disappearing
ear hearing
out of sight
music less
shadow fallen
fallen light
shapes music
beneath

What silence has
to say
        words
mean to
see

STORY

My six-year old wanted to read, so I handed her a book by
Robert Lax:

> one stone
> one stone
> one stone
>
> one stone
> one stone...

When she'd read out most of the poems, she looked at her
mother and me sitting at the table.

'He's a very strange poet! We should find his number and give
him a call.'

I said I wrote him a letter once, but on the day I was to send it
discovered through an old friend of his he had just died.

After Eva read the book, I remembered that morning she'd
written the following on my typewriter, as if her words had
predicted she would read him:

> I (do) do not
> I (do) do not
> I (do) do not
> I (do) do not
> I (do) do not

AFTER

Imagination
is memory
looking back on
what will be.

THEN

And nothing in the world exists
or has ever existed
except this moment
which does not and never will
have existed
in another moment
from now

Of all the lines written in the margins of Carlos Drummond de Andrade's *In the Middle of the Road* the only ones thirty years later I don't disagree with.

STONE

Because once written words remain,
take care what you write.

Each word stays where it is,
proclaiming what's no longer true.

TRANSPARENT

The trick is to
say something
without using
a word to
say it

since words
find it
impossible to
say anything
not themselves

STUDY

for Michael Palmer

He means to
to say he
means to
say to hear
to hear said
it is not
a thing a
thing said
heard it
is not a
thing
a crack a
crack in
the floorboards
it means
he says say
mouth at the window
mouth at the
window
pain a
pulse it
is a pulse
it is
no
one's

Grasping what is
to utter how
into a shape
that might yet last
the breath we lose.

READING

Reading Jean Daive on his friend Paul Celan: struck by this sentence: *a stranger to nothing in this world.* Looking back through the book, I can't find those words anywhere. Yet swear I read it this afternoon, sitting on the bench in the garden, while my daughter Lana slept upstairs and the house was otherwise empty. It was a line that pierced me. Perhaps because my first reaction to it, however brief, was positive. Then the shock, the revulsion: that someone could say that about another person; that it could be true.

Within
every tale
told

an untold
tale

the words

— very quietly —

tell themselves

CIRCULAR STUDY

for John Wells

Circles and the
shapes of circles not
exactly there
there perhaps suggested

a suggestion of circles faintly
drawn impressed imagined even

only half circled say half a

some time one edges ever over
slightly toward and into light-
ly one other not
one circle and another

some half circles

the shape of
lines
not there
                still
                seen

SHAPE

It's not that I
presume you are

here listening
just because I

am here speaking.
That's not it.

Perhaps no
one is here.

There are words,
or such is

apparent. But words
do not mean

someone is saying them
or someone is

listening. Any more
than a chair means

someone must be
present to sit

in it, or even that
it was made

for the purpose
of sitting.

PERSONA

for Fernando Pessoa

It's probably true healthy people do not write poems, or —
rather — do not need to. Write them, they might. The same
way they might keep a cat, or use a hammer to nail wood.

*

I never was the one I thought I was
being each time I approached another
whose arrival announced the departure
of whoever it was being both.

*

He remembered so little of what was his life he had begun to
believe that it wasn't his life he had lived at all. Yet, if that were
the case, wouldn't he remember details from whoever's life he
had lived?

*

Of the many that I was
no proof remains
any of us were
more than figments
another imagined who

remained unknown
to each of us —
including himself.
Whoever I now am
is just as likely
not to exist
in any future
that happens to be
waiting for the one
becoming me
to fill. Whether this
helps explain why
these words are
not being written by
the one writing them
(or not being read
by the one reading them)
is for another
(so far unknown)
to decide.

What you have
here to use
uses you
beyond what
use you make
of it.

CORRESPONDENCE

From the last letter I wrote him
John Levy said he could see
these lines becoming a
poem:

Everyone has
gone swimming to the pool.

I am here.

I couldn't, but in his letter I found:

Early grey-blue dawn here,
clear sky, no
coyotes
yipping at the moment
in a frenzy, having
chased down
or chasing down
small prey
(rabbits, rats, probably birds,
cats, small
dogs, etc.).

What I like most is
neither of us
wrote either.

Nor this.

AFFINITY

for Roger Snell

Analogy of Escape was the first book I read by Keith Waldrop. One poem in particular struck me: a single line, in parentheses:

ACTUAL

(Often, in the mirror, I see *one image too many*.)

Sometime before or after reading this I must've purloined its title, if not more, for the following:

ACTUAL

At the back of
my head

some
thing crouching

I sit
down with

Slipped into the pages of the book, I found a cleanly folded sheet of paper. Printed on the sheet, a three-line poem:

Affinity

Light on wet branches takes the shape of the tree
a light tree
two minds speeding by glitter instantly

I'd no idea whether this poem was originally meant as part of the book — there could've been a similar sheet tucked into every copy. Unlikely, but I found the idea compelling.

Or, someone placed the poem there. (The book was bought second hand; I don't remember where.)

The lines could well be by Waldrop; a hint, also, to three of my own —

light

shape of

the street

Even a harkening back to *The Light Tree and Fourteenth Beauty*.

It's several years ago now I bought the book. I can't say for sure whether I found the sheet of paper folded in it or whether, at a later, now forgotten date, I placed it there.

I wanted the least and they punished me with more

Did I read the poem or did I write it?

* * *

I was working on something last night — I needed a longer piece to break up the reading I'm preparing — thinking whoever the audience is, they wouldn't want to hear too many small poems without a change of pace. Decided to use that old letter to you — about the poem I found in Keith Waldrop's book. As I was connected to the internet, I thought to type in the first line.

The poem was written by an Irishman, Randolph Healy. But everything is not exactly as it appears. The three lines are not a separate entity, but one verse of a much longer work. A couple of words are also different: whereas the 'original' reads *two minds speeding by glitter instantly*, Healy's reads: *six minds speeding by trace it instantly*. No idea what the change from *six* to *two minds* might signify, but otherwise I prefer my version.

Healy's poem, *Scales*, was published in 1998; Waldrop's book the year before.

I've never read Healy, but a week ago I picked up a couple of books by poets whose names I knew but whose work I didn't. I hadn't found the time to look, but remembered one was a selection of his work. Sure enough, the longer poem containing 'my' poem is the final piece in the book.

It also seems there's a recording of him reading the poem. Would be interesting to hear which he reads.

This morning I looked more closely at my copy of *Analogy of Escape*. What I had always thought an inscription of ownership, quite indecipherable, I could now make out clearly: a dedication, reading: *For Randolph, from Keith*.

READING

Remember
these words

know more
than you

you came here
for a purpose

no word
could give.

Knowing it is wrong
doesn't mean it's wrong.
Any more than knowing
it's right means it is
right.
　　　Knowing isn't is.
Only thinks it is.

After thinking I am not
who I thought myself to be
I couldn't imagine being
anyone else.

THIS

Whatever else it is a poem
is often nothing

more than thinking
there's something there to be

found when there's
nothing but thinking so.

I searched in the silence
for the word

that would tell me
why I searched for a word

in the silence
to be told a reason

to search for what
could not be found

A WAY

Your absence is
the silence
to say this
toward your not
being here.

Saying it again is not
saying it again it is
not repeated nothing is
nothing said again is
repeated one word after
another word one and the same
word after one word
the same is not the same
is not again said
saying it the same word
is not the same
is not the sound is not
it is another sound
the word it makes is
another sounding
something different some
thing other sounded
sounding something
other another
another it is it
is not the same
not again
nothing is
each time
once
committed

        nothing
        repeated is

So much here
being not
ever known
other than
that was it
which is gone.

the sun on my bed
is an orange — I'll save it
in my hat for you

WAYS

for Cid Corman

each road's relentless
to who travels
            thinking to
actually   arrive.

      *

it means what it does
the doing of
         being us
eventually
     done.

      *

I talk
to listen to

the sense of it
silence

never quite gets
said.

      *

no point
        in asking
the answer to be
            more than
it is
    which we do

      *

the original
act
    was a word
            unspoken
we each are
      to say.

      *

inexplicable —
what you must explain
               to see
you're
      the meaning of.

      *

the invention of
silence
      took place after we
invented
      language.

      *

walking backwards to
what's still ahead
                    to keep what
you will have
            to lose.

*

all I think to say
says what
            of all I think to
mean
        the saying for.

*

no meaning to loss
beyond
            the meaning you have
being here
            to lose.

*

language invented us
to speak what it never
knew
we had to say.

*

forgetting to say
what must be said

is our way
to keep on talking.

*

the world has its own
living to do
                that doesn't
include
        always
                us.

*

perpetually
postponed
                the now
                        that language
makes present
                as past.

*

it takes a while to
recognise
                how much is gone
you still have
                to go.

*

the circumference
to the circle
we are

we never
get to
see.

*

eventually you
will know
            what it was you did
at least
            not come for.

*

to say the nothing
there is
to say

all these words
are needed
to fail.

*

life
    can
  easily
do
   without
        us
   how
      ever
much
  we
     pretend
  not.

      *

what we say   amounts to   a single syllable —

b r e a t h l e s s l y p r o n o u n c e d

      *

no one watching knew
the whole show
        was made up from
those made
      to watch it.

      *

to be truly
            blank
a page
            must have
                        — visible —
words
            not
                        written
            there.

                        *

to say enough to
never have to say again
never is
            what's said.

                        *

it takes a lifetime
to find the one answer

there is
no question to.

TO

*Ian
Hamilton
Finlay*

SEA

a wave a boat   .
a wave

WAVES

      black
rocks
      white

RAIN VARIATIONS

I

In the rain it's
the cold not silent
itself silence
the rain a little
cold a little
silent falling
into both

II

In the rain
the cold
itself
the rain
cold a
silent
into

III

In the silence
rain it's
the cold not
silent itself
the cold a
silence a
rain

IV

Into both
silent falling
cold a little
rain a little
silence itself
the cold not
rain falling
silent

V

In the rain
the cold not silent
the cold
itself silence
itself
the rain a
little rain
cold a
cold silent falling
into

VI

In the rain it's
the silence
the cold not silent
the cold
a rain it's
itself silence
itself

the cold not
the rain a little
the rain
silent itself
cold a little
the cold a
cold silence
falling

VII

In the rain it's
the rain
in the silence
into both
the cold not silent
the cold
rain it's
silent falling
itself silence
itself
the cold not
cold a little
the rain a little
the rain
silent itself
rain a little
cold a little
cold a
silent falling
silence itself
rain a little
into both
the cold

not into
in silence
silent
falling

LOST

Still looking
for the piece

of that word
that fell off

the last time
I used it —

thinking it
might explain

what happened
next or say

what didn't

THEORY OF COMPOSITION

There is a rumour this poem never existed.

Others maintain the only known copy — scrawled in a childish hand on the back of a used aerogramme — was lost before anyone had a chance to read it.

A few agree that at one time the poem did exist, but they insist it was never written down.

Those who believe a poem can cast a shadow, or under the correct circumstances, emit a faint light, may regard this note as proof of whatever notion they seek to defend.

MOUNTAINS & RIVERS

T'AO CH'IEN

his
poems
complain

the way
not found

he walked

*

day light
firefly

nothing
much

*

SHINE

sun
black
cormorant
wings

*

her
comb
come
use
less
ly
up
on

＊

moon
on
water

no
closer

＊

Old Ts'ang K'o
invented
writing for
us to know

UNFOUND

Sorry, but you are
looking for
something that
isn't here.

MEANING

It's not to
say anything

but to think
something

not thought
before it

is said
makes this

what
it is

BOOK OF RESEMBLANCES

I found this line jotted in pencil at the bottom of page 125 of 'The Book of Resemblances': *'To be what flees from being. 30.10.98.'*

The thought must have come to me due to reading, on the same page, the following line (a line I partly wrote over): *'To read what flees from reading'*. The words I noted down would doubtless never have existed without the push that Jabès gave to my thinking.

Creation? Theft? Or, I found it there because I was looking there.

As I was this morning — eight years after last reading the book.

I feel no desire to claim the line, or any of these subsequent to it.

SIDESHOW

Words are not for communication
else there'd be more of it.
It could even seem they're here to
make communication more difficult,
making us believe we can communicate,
the more we fail to.
                    Like belief in God
demotes the devil to a supporting role.

What is happening
when this is happening

is what this
happens to be.

The shape of faith is the
shape of faith is the shape of a

weapon

always
always has been

the shape of faith is a weapon defends it
a weapon attacks who have no faith

who have another faith
the shape of faith is a weapon attacks

attacks who have no faith
who have another faith

the shape of faith attacks
is a weapon

the shape of faith is not peace
it is death   the shape of

faith

a faith of weapons

attacks who have another
who have no

faith

shape of a
weapon

What I mean to say
and what I say
are different things.

Always this
wasn't it.

GRATITUDE

for Fadhila Chabbi

Wherever I walked dust covered my tracks

Whatever I made fell to a thousand pieces

Whatever I said was lost in the wind

Whoever I loved loved nothing in the end

Whoever I created vanished the same

What it is
in language

condemns us
to misuse,

we are